JUN - 7 2016

Readers' Theater: How to Put on a Production

Pickles and Parks

A Readers' Theater Script and Guide

Looking Glass Library

An Imprint of Magic Wagon
abdopublishing.com

By Nancy K. Wallace   Illustrated by Lucy Fleming

To Lorraine Ranchod, who made Ellwood City's Earth Day Celebrations awesome! —NKW

abdopublishing.com

Published by Magic Wagon, a division of ABDO, PO Box 398166, Minneapolis, Minnesota 55439.
Copyright © 2016 by Abdo Consulting Group, Inc. International copyrights reserved in all countries. No part of this book may be reproduced in any form without written permission from the publisher. Looking Glass Library™ is a trademark and logo of Magic Wagon.

Printed in the United States of America, North Mankato, Minnesota.
042015
092015

THIS BOOK CONTAINS RECYCLED MATERIALS

Written by Nancy K. Wallace
Illustrations by Lucy Fleming
Edited by Heidi M.D. Elston, Megan M. Gunderson & Bridget O'Brien
Designed by Laura Mitchell

Library of Congress Cataloging-in-Publication Data

Wallace, Nancy K.
 Pickles and parks : a readers' theater script and guide / by Nancy K. Wallace ; illustrated by Lucy Fleming.
   pages cm. -- (Readers' theater: how to put on a production set 2)
 ISBN 978-1-62402-116-9
1. Earth Day--Juvenile drama. 2. Theater--Production and direction--Juvenile literature. 3. Readers' theater--Juvenile literature. I. Fleming, Lucy, illustrator. II. Title.
 PS3623.A4436P53 2016
 812'.6--dc23
                        2015003775

Table of Contents

Celebrate with a Play!

Everyone loves holidays! Some schools and libraries hold programs or assemblies to commemorate special occasions. This series offers fun plays to help celebrate six different holidays at your school or library. You can even sell tickets and use your play as a fund-raiser.

Readers' theater can be done very simply. The performers sit on stools or chairs onstage. They don't have to memorize their lines. They just read them.

Adapted readers' theater looks more like a regular play. The stage includes scenery and props. The performers wear makeup and costumes. They move around to show the action. But, they still carry their scripts.

Readers' theater scripts can also be used for puppet shows. The performers stand behind a curtain, move the puppets, and read their scripts.

Find a place large enough to put on a play. An auditorium with a stage is ideal. A classroom will work, too. Choose a date and ask permission to use the space. Advertise your play with posters and flyers. Place them around your school and community. Tell your friends and family. Everyone enjoys watching a fun performance!

Tickets and Playbills

Tickets and playbills can be handwritten or designed on a computer. Be sure tickets include the title of the play. They should list the date, time, and location of the performance.

A playbill is a printed program. The front of a playbill has the title of the play, the date, and the time. The cast and crew are listed inside. Be sure to have enough playbills for the audience and cast. Pass them out at the door as the audience enters.

The Crew

Next, a crew is needed. The show can't go on without these important people! Some jobs can be combined for a small show.

Director — organizes everyone and everything in the show.

Costume Designer — designs and borrows or makes all the costumes.

Stage Manager — makes sure everything runs smoothly.

Lighting Designer — runs spotlights and other lighting.

Set Designer — plans and makes scenery.

Prop Manager — finds, makes, and keeps track of props.

Special Effects Crew — takes care of sound and other special effects.

Sets

At a readers' theater production, the performers can sit on stools at the front of the room. An adapted readers' theater production or full play will require sets and props. A set is the background that creates the setting for each scene. A prop is an item the actors use onstage.

Scene 1 takes place in the school cafeteria. Paint a cardboard backdrop for the cafeteria, showing additional tables or a lunch line. You will need a table and four chairs. Add a recycling can!

Scene 2 and **scene 3** are in Mrs. Moreno's classroom. Use a large teacher's desk or table for both scenes. Put different props on the desk to help show the passage of time.

Scene 4 needs a backdrop of a park with trees and bushes. Include a park bench or two in the scene. If possible, place tables toward the back of the stage to display the students' projects.

Props

- Reusable lunch bags
- Reusable water bottles
- 2 cookies
- 2 granola bars
- Sandwich
- Papers, books, and pens

for Mrs. Moreno's desk
- 2 trash bags stuffed with newspaper
- Basket
- Seed packets stapled to recipe cards
- Cooler

- Fake Popsicles
- Craft supplies based on which activities students choose to show in scene 4
- Sign that says "Hug a Tree Every Day" on one side and "The End" on the other

The Cast

Decide who will play each part. Each person in the cast will need a script. All of the performers should practice their lines. Reading lines aloud over and over will help the performers learn them. *Pickles and Parks* needs the following cast:

Logan — a student

Zack — Logan's best friend

Grace — a student

Ella — a student

Mrs. Moreno — a teacher

Extra actors for scenes 2 and 4

Makeup and Costumes

Makeup artists have a big job! Every cast member wears makeup. And, stage makeup needs to be brighter and heavier than regular makeup. Buy several basic shades of mascara, foundation, blush, and lipstick. Apply with a new cotton ball or swab for each cast member to avoid spreading germs.

Costume designers set the scene just as much as set designers. They borrow costumes or adapt old clothing for each character. Ask adults for help finding and sewing costumes.

Most of the performers in this play can wear regular clothes they would wear to school. There is one exception.

Logan needs a tree costume! He should be able to pull the costume over his school clothes for an easy costume change. Use a hot glue gun to attach real or silk leaves to brown fabric. You can also print realistic leaves or cut some out of construction paper.

Rehearsals and Stage Directions

After you decide to put on a play, it is important to set up a rehearsal schedule. Choose a time everyone can attend, such as after school or on weekends. Try to have at least five rehearsals before the performance.

Everyone should practice together as a team, even though individual actors will be reading their own scripts. This will help the play sound like a conversation, instead of separate lines. Onstage, actors should act like their characters even when they aren't speaking.

In the script, stage directions are in parentheses. They are given from the performer's point of view, not the audience's. Actors face the audience when performing, so left is on their left and right is on their right.

Some theater terms may be unfamiliar:

Curtains — the main curtain at the front of the stage.

House — the area in which the audience sits.

Wings — the part of the stage on either side that the audience can't see.

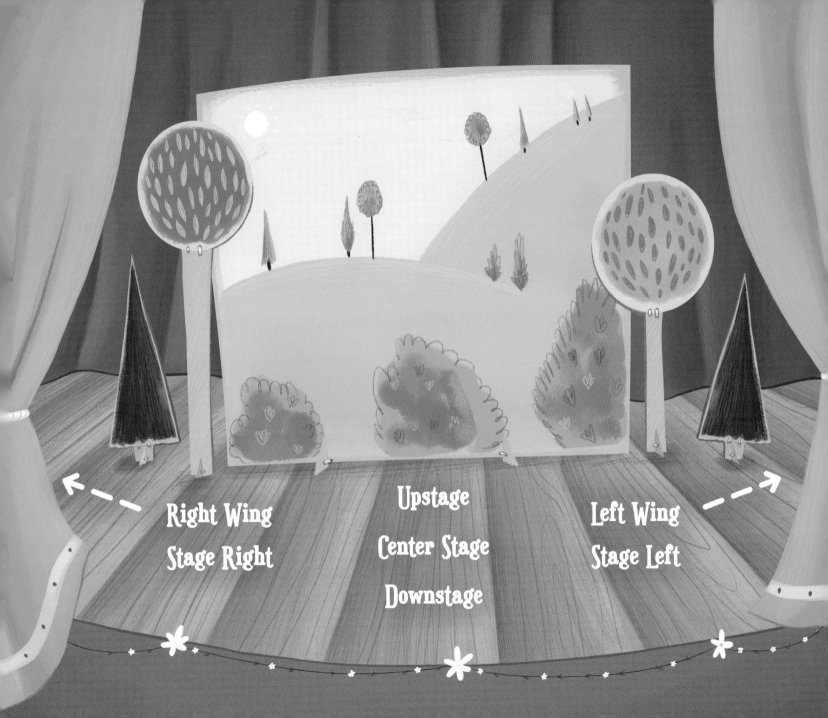

Right Wing
Stage Right

Upstage
Center Stage
Downstage

Left Wing
Stage Left

Script: *Pickles and Parks*
Scene 1: The Cafeteria

(Logan, Zack, Grace, and Ella sit at a table, center stage, eating lunch together. Use real food for props so they can eat as they talk. Place two students at the back of the table and one on each end, angled toward the audience. Have a recycling container at stage left.)

Grace: What are you doing for your Earth Day project, Zack?

Zack: Mrs. Moreno mentioned growing your own food, so I asked Bob at the hardware store if they had any old seeds left over from last year. I just wanted to make a chart for a small space garden and glue the seeds on it to show people what they look like. But, he gave me this humongous box *full* of seed packets, and he said the seeds are still good. So I can actually plant them, too!

Logan: Yeah, Zack could plant half the town in vegetables! We could have beans in all the parking lots, a pumpkin patch on Main Street, and a zucchini in every flowerpot!

Zack: And cucumber vines on all the lampposts!

Ella: Ooh, do you have extra cucumber seeds?

Zack: Tons!

Ella: Since we talked about making food from scratch, I made a flyer with my grandma's recipe for homemade pickles. Could I have some seeds to staple to my recipes?

Zack: Sure!

Grace: I made recipes, too! Mom and I experimented with different kinds of natural fruit Popsicles. I like raspberry best. They don't have any added sugar, and they taste so good!

Logan: *(Rubbing his hands together.)* Yum! We'll all come over for samples later.

Grace: We made a lot. Our freezer is full of them!

Zack: I wish I had one right now.

Grace: *(Holds up a cookie.)* I have an extra oatmeal cookie. Do you want that?

Zack: Sure! Thanks!

Logan: What about me?

Ella: *(Handing Logan a granola bar.)* I have two granola bars. You can have one.

Logan: Thanks, Ella!

Ella: What's your project, Logan?

Logan: Since we talked about reforestation in class, my dad and I found a place online where you can order 100 free trees. I'm going to give one to everybody in our class, but I don't have a clue what we're going to do with the rest of them.

Zack: We all have a gazillion samples! I feel like all we do is think about Earth Day and our projects these days!

Logan: Yeah, but we must be the only ones. You won't believe what my dad did last night. He put three cardboard boxes in the trash!

Ella: You're kidding!

Logan: I'm not! I watched him do it. He said he didn't have time to break them down and recycle them.

Grace: We hear about reducing, reusing, and recycling all the time at school. Maybe everyone in town needs to hear about it, too.

Zack: Do you remember that movie they showed us in science class where Earth was one big pile of trash?

Logan: *(Enthusiastically.)* Oh yeah! The one where everyone had to live on a spaceship and they just floated around on big recliners and played video games? That was cool!

Zack: Sometimes, I think that might really happen.

Logan: Because of my dad?

Zack: Because they teach us this stuff at school, but some people don't actually do it.

Grace: Maybe people have lost interest in some of the things Earth Day stands for. It started way back in 1970. That's forever ago.

Ella: We could put all our projects in a book.

Zack: But how many people would read it?

Logan: Our parents would. That would take care of my dad and the cardboard boxes!

Zack: I guess that's a start. But we should think of something bigger.

Logan: What if we included the community? We could invite everyone to come the day we present our projects.

Zack: Let's ask Mrs. Moreno what she thinks.

Grace: We'd better hurry! Her next class starts in ten minutes.

(Zack, Grace, and Ella gather their things, stand up, and exit stage left.)

Logan: Hey, I'm not done with my sandwich! It's my idea, guys! Wait! *(Logan grabs his sandwich and lunch bag and runs off stage left.)*

Scene 2: Mrs. Moreno's Classroom

(Scenes 2 and 3 should take place in front of the curtain or in front of freestanding cardboard panels. The setup for the park in scene 4 can take place behind the curtain. Mrs. Moreno stands by her desk at center stage. Zack, Grace, and Ella rush in from stage right, Logan trails behind, still eating his sandwich.)

Mrs. Moreno: *(Smiling.)* Whoa, aren't you guys in the wrong classroom? You've already had my class once today.

Logan: We just need to ask a question. Do you think we could plan an Earth Day festival?

Mrs. Moreno: Here at school?

Zack, **Logan**, **Grace**, and **Ella:** Yeah!

Grace: Everyone came up with such great Earth Day projects. We'd like to share them with the whole community. Could we do it in the cafeteria or the auditorium?

Mrs. Moreno: That's a very good idea, but I don't think either of those places is large enough for that many people. Could we just invite your parents?

Logan: I think everyone needs to hear about Earth Day! Even my parents don't always recycle.

Ella: *(Tentatively.)* Could we use the park?

Mrs. Moreno: What if it rains? Earth Day is April 22, and April showers . . .

Logan: There are picnic shelters.

Mrs. Moreno: Okay, let's slow down. We'd have to ask for permission to use the park. The city controls who gets to use it. Something may already be scheduled for that day.

Ella: My mom works at City Hall. I can ask her to check.

Mrs. Moreno: Before you ask her, let's think about this a little more. What kinds of activities would you include?

Logan: We'd use our own projects, but we'd also include recycling, upcycling, living green, caring for wildlife, and . . .

Mrs. Moreno: *(Interrupts.)* Wow! It sounds like you have a lot of really good ideas, but a festival that big would take a lot of planning. What if we just include your Earth Day projects? That would be a good way to start. We could ask other classes to participate, too. And we'll need more adults to help us if we're even considering holding it in the park.

Grace: I'll bet Mr. Bess at the library would help. The library always makes a display for Earth Week.

Mrs. Moreno: Okay, let's do this in steps. First, Ella, can you ask your mom about using the community park? Second, Grace, will you ask Mr. Bess at the library if he will help?

Logan: *(Giving Zack a high five.)* Yay! We're going to make this happen!

Mrs. Moreno: Don't get too excited. Let's see if we can use the park and get some volunteers first.

Logan: I'll ask Mrs. MacMurdo if she would help. We've been doing art projects for Earth Day, too.

Zack: Bob, who gave me the seeds at the hardware store, said he would be happy to help the school with a project. He probably wasn't thinking it would be this soon, but I'll ask him, too.

Mrs. Moreno: I'm so glad you kids are really enthusiastic about this! Could we meet again Friday before school?

Logan, **Zack**, **Grace**, and **Ella:** Sure!

(Other students begin to enter from stage right, carrying their books.)

Mrs. Moreno: Okay, I'll see you then. You'd better hurry! You'll be late for your next class!

Logan: See you Friday!

Grace: Bye!

(Logan, Zack, Ella, and Grace exit stage right.)

Scene 3: Mrs. Moreno's Classroom

(Same setup as scene 2. Mrs. Moreno, Grace, and Ella are already gathered around Mrs. Moreno's desk.)

Mrs. Moreno: Where are the boys?

Grace: They'll be here. They're just always late.

(Logan and Zack enter from stage right carrying trash bags.)

Ella: Ew! What is *that*?

Logan: What does it look like?

Ella: Trash?

Logan: Yep! Zack and I went over to the park this morning before school, and we picked up two bags of trash in fifteen minutes. We have fast-food containers, paper bags, cups, and a bunch of other junk.

Mrs. Moreno: We can't hold Earth Day in a park filled with trash! It sounds like we need to educate the public about littering, too.

Zack: Yep!

Ella: I asked my mom, and she said we can use the park. April 22 is free! She penciled us in, but we have to write a letter and make a formal request.

Mrs. Moreno: I'll do that today and drop it off after school.

Grace: I think we should ask our whole class to help clean up the park.

Logan: That would be great. It would take forever for us to do it ourselves!

Mrs. Moreno: I'll ask the principal today. Maybe we can schedule a clean-up day next Saturday. Did you find any other volunteers to help on Earth Day?

Grace: Mr. Bess and two other librarians will come. They're planning a craft table to make nature journals out of wallpaper samples. That's recycling *and* upcycling!

Mrs. Moreno: That's great!

Zack: Bob from the hardware store is donating potting soil and little pots for the seeds. He said he would set up a booth and get one of his coworkers to help him.

Logan: And Mrs. MacMurdo said she'll do a craft table with leaf prints. Her son Carter said he'll help, too.

Zack: My dad's company offered to provide free electronics recycling. So people can bring their old computers, phones, TVs . . . all kinds of stuff!

Mrs. Moreno: (*Looking pleased.*) You kids are amazing! This is coming along nicely.

Ella: I think it would be fun if we did something special for the preschoolers.

Logan: Zack and I are working on that. But it's a surprise. You'll have to wait until Earth Day to find out.

(*Zack and Logan exit stage right.*)

Mrs. Moreno: I wonder what that's all about.

Scene 4: Earth Day

(Set the stage with real or artificial trees and plants. Use park benches if available. Put two tables toward the back of the stage with different craft projects on them. Have lots of students walking around the tables, pretending to look at things and talk about them. Grace should have a cooler beside her and be holding a fake Popsicle.)

Mrs. Moreno: What a wonderful Earth Day festival! We should do it every year. Maybe next time, we could include those displays on wildlife sanctuaries and living green.

Ella: You sound like Logan! He's already planning next year's festival.

Grace: Did you see those bird feeders the fifth graders made out of upcycled plastic bottles and wooden spoons? I want to make one for my grandfather.

Ella: I like those, too! Wow, there are a ton of people here today! *(She holds out a basket with seed packets stapled to recipe cards.)* I've given out almost 200 pickle recipes.

Mrs. Moreno: Maybe those seeds will encourage more people to have vegetable gardens this summer! *(She turns toward Grace.)* Your Popsicles are a real hit, too, Grace!

Grace: Thanks! I only have three left.

Ella: One of the librarians is helping kids build fairy houses out of moss and twigs. They are sooo cute! I hope I have time to make one before this is over at two o'clock.

Grace: I can pass out your pickle recipes if you want to go now.

Ella: Okay, thanks! *(Ella exits stage right.)*

Mrs. Moreno: Grace, who contacted the lady with the alpacas? It was wonderful that she could bring them for the children to see. People seem really interested in the yarn she brought and the knitted projects, too. Maybe next year we can have more displays on natural fibers.

Grace: I don't know. Maybe the alpacas were the surprise Logan was talking about.

Mrs. Moreno: Speaking of Logan, I haven't seen either Logan or Zack for quite a while. Do you know where they are?

Grace: They were here the whole time we were setting up. *(She looks around.)* Logan's dad is over there passing out trees, but I don't see Logan.

Mrs. Moreno: That's strange.

Grace: It's a big park, and there are a lot of people. Maybe they're here and we just haven't seen them.

Ella: *(Runs back onstage from stage right.)* Oh my gosh, wait till you see Logan!

(Zack and Logan enter from stage right. Logan is dressed as a tree, and Zack is carrying a sign that says "Hug a Tree Every Day!" Grace and Ella start to laugh.)

Grace: That's the funniest thing I've ever seen!

Logan: Laugh all you want. You won't believe how many times I've had my picture taken today!

Zack: Little kids love his costume! They just run up and hug him!

Mrs. Moreno: I love your costume, too, Logan! This has been a really great Earth Day festival.

Zack: Yeah, it's the best Earth Day ever! I can't wait till next year!

(Zack flips the sign around to reveal it says . . .)

The End

Adapting Readers' Theater Scripts

Readers' theater can be done very simply. Performers just read their lines from scripts. They don't have to memorize them! And, they don't have to move around. The performers sit on chairs or stools while reading their parts.

Adapted Readers' Theater: This looks more like a regular play. The performers wear makeup and costumes. The stage has scenery and props. The cast moves around to show the action. Performers can still read from their scripts.

A Puppet Show: Some schools and libraries have puppet collections. Or students can create puppets. Students make the puppets be the actors. They read their scripts for their puppets.

Teaching Guides

Readers' Theater Teaching Guides are available online at **abdopublishing.com**. Each guide includes printable scripts, reading levels for each character, and additional production tips for each play. Get yours today!

Websites

To learn more about Readers' Theater, visit **booklinks.abdopublishing.com**. These links are routinely monitored and updated to provide the most current information available.